D1358978

SELECTED FROM

Contemporary American Plays

VOLUME TWO

Supplementary material by Lori Gurr and
the staff of Literacy Volunteers
of New York City

WRITERS' VOICES
Literacy Volunteers of New York City

SELECTED FROM CONTEMPORARY AMERICAN PLAYS, VOLUME TWO was made possible by grants from the Hale Matthews Foundation, Uris Brothers Foundation and The Shubert Organization, Inc.

Supplementary materials © 1992 by Literacy Volunteers of New York City Inc.

Writers' Voices is a series of books published by Literacy Volunteers of New York City Inc., 121 Avenue of the Americas, New York, NY 10013. The words, "Writers' Voices," are a trademark of Literacy Volunteers of New York City.

Cover designed by Paul Davis Studio; interior designed by Barbara Huntley.

LVNYC is an affiliate of Literacy Volunteers of America.

ACKNOWLEDGMENTS

Literacy Volunteers of New York City gratefully acknowledges the generous support of the following foundations and corporations that made the publication of Selected from Contemporary American Plays, Volume Two possible: the Hale Matthews Foundation, Uris Brothers Foundation and The Shubert Organization, Inc.

This book could not have been realized without the kind and generous cooperation of the playwrights and their representatives: Arthur Miller and his publisher, Viking Penguin, a division of Penguin Books USA Inc.; Lonne Elder III and his publisher, Farrar, Straus and Giroux, Inc.; Beth Henley and her publisher, New American Library, a division of Penguin Books USA Inc.; Lynne Alvarez and her agent, Helen Merrill, Ltd.; David Mamet and his agent, Rosenstone/Wender; Terrence McNally and his publisher, Villard Books, a division of Random House, Inc.; Harvey Fierstein and his publisher, New American Library, a division of Penguin Books USA Inc.; Spike Lee and his representatives, Franklin, Garbus, Klein and Selz.

We deeply appreciate the contributions of the following suppliers: Cam Steel Rule Die Works Inc. (steel cutting die for display); Domtar Industries Inc. (text stock); Westchester Book Composition Inc. (text typesetting); Horizon Paper Company (cover stock); MCUSA (display header); Delta Corrugated Container (corrugated display); Verilen Graphics Inc. (cover color separations); and Offset Paperback Manufacturers, Inc., A Bertelsmann Company (cover and text printing and binding).

For their guidance, support and hard work, we are indebted to the LVNYC Board of Directors' Publishing Committee: James E. Galton, Marvel Comics Ltd.; Virginia Barber, Virginia Barber Literary Agency, Inc.; Doris Bass, Scholastic Inc.; Jeff Brown; Jerry Butler, William Morrow & Company, Inc.; George P. Davidson, Ballantine Books; Joy M. Gannon, St. Martin's Press; Walter Kiechel, *Fortune*; Geraldine E. Rhoads; Virginia Rice, Reader's Digest; Martin Singerman, News America Publishing, Inc.; James L. Stanko, James Money Management, Inc.; and F. Robert Stein, Pryor, Cashman, Sherman & Flynn.

Thanks also to Joy M. Gannon and Julia Weil of St. Martin's Press for producing this book; Arnold Dolin, Arnold Schaab, Michael Greaves, Elise Pritchard, Florence B. Eichen and Lisa Davis for help in obtaining permissions; Helen Morris for reviewing plays for selection; Lori Gum for her skill and diligence in the research and writing of the supplementary material for this book; Carol Fein for her thoughtful copyediting and suggestions; and to Pam Johnson for proofreading. Thanks also to F. Robert Stein for legal advice.

Our thanks to Paul Davis Studio and Myrna Davis, Paul Davis, Lisa Mazur, Chalkley Calderwood and Alex Ginns for their inspired design of the covers of these books. Thanks also to Barbara Huntley for her sensitive design of the interior of this book.

CONTENTS

NOTE TO THE READER

"Books can give you a lot. You can live a hundred lives instead of just one."
—Arthur Miller, playwright

Playwriting is a special form of writing. It is meant to be heard as well as read.

Every writer has a special voice. That is why we call our series *Writers' Voices*. We chose the eight playwrights in *Selected from Contemporary American Plays, Volume Two* because each playwright's special voice can be clearly heard. You will hear it through the story each has chosen to tell and the way his or her characters speak and act.

WHAT IS A PLAY?

A play is a story written to be seen and heard on a stage or screen. The playwright creates characters who tell their story through words and actions. When you see or read a play, you watch the characters' lives unfold.

READING A PLAY

Many people enjoy reading plays. Some people enjoy reading them because plays are mostly dialogue (the lines the actors speak) and action without a lot of description. Still others hope to write their own plays and read plays to get ideas for their own work. Some people may have seen a play or movie in a theater and read the play because they are curious about the differences between what they saw and what the playwright wrote.

Reading a play is very different from seeing a play. In a sense, you must be the director: you must make the play come alive for yourself.

Think about the play's setting (the description of the time and place of the play). You can find out about the setting in the Editors' Introduction to each play. Try to imagine how it might look. If the play is set in a small apartment, you could imagine the kind of furniture it might have. If the play is set on a beach, you could picture the palm trees and water.

Think about the characters. Try to imagine how they might look. Are they tall or short, fat or thin, young or old? How do they dress? You might even picture someone you know to make a character come alive.

As you read the dialogue, try imagining how it might be spoken. Does the character have a particular kind of accent? Does she speak loudly or softly, fast or slowly? Is he being sarcastic or funny?

Think about how the characters move and what they are doing as they speak or listen. The playwright will tell you when characters enter or exit the stage, but she may only give you a few clues to their other actions.

HOW TO READ THE SPECIAL FORMAT OF A PLAY

A play is set up differently on the page than other kinds of writing. That is because its first purpose is to help the director and the actors quickly locate the information they need to perform it.

The dialogue is easy to find. The character's name appears in capital letters and the words that he or she is supposed to say follow the name. For example:

SAL: Extra cheese is two dollars.

Stage directions and other information that is important to the actors or director are set in italic type. The italic type signals to the actor that this should not be spoken aloud. This information often appears in brackets to help set it apart from the dialogue. For example:

[*Sound of a key in the lock. All heads turn.*]

HOW TO READ THIS BOOK

Before Reading

• Think about why you want to read this book. Do you like reading plays? Do you hope to write a play?

• Look at the Contents page. Decide which plays you want to read and in what order you want to read them.

During Reading

• Begin your reading with the Editors' Introduction to each selection. It will explain something about the play and its characters.

• Think about what you know about the play before you begin reading the dialogue. Try to picture the characters and setting.

• There may be words or names that are difficult to read. Keep reading to see if the meaning becomes clear. If it doesn't, ask someone for the word. Or look up the word in a dictionary.

• Ask yourself questions as you read. For example: Do I believe this play or character? Why?

After Reading

• Think about what you have read. Did you identify with any of the characters in the play? Did the situation make you see any of your own experiences in a new light?

• Talk with others about your thoughts.

Reading Aloud

• You might also want to read the lines aloud, as if you were an actor. You could experiment with saying the lines in different ways. You might even read the selection aloud with a group of people. Each person could take a different part.

• If you read the selections with a group, discuss the reading afterward. Each person could talk about what he thought his character looked like and what motivated the character's words and actions.

Each selection in this book can be read and enjoyed separately. You might also want to discuss what is the same or different about the plays and the playwrights. For example, Arthur Miller, Harvey Fierstein, Beth Henley and Lonne Elder III all examine family relationships but in very different ways. How do the characters view the different members of their families? Terrence McNally and Lynne Alvarez create very special moods in their selections using only two characters. What do the characters say or do that helps create this mood? The selections by David Mamet and Spike Lee were written for the screen as opposed to the stage. How do they build tension using the eye of the camera?

We have also included a special interview with the playwright Arthur Miller on page 60. In it, he shares some of his thoughts about his writing. We hope this will give you some ideas and inspiration for your own writing.

Selected from Contemporary American Plays and *Selected from Contemporary American Plays, Volume Two* are meant to introduce you to the joys of reading plays. Also available is *How to Write a Play*, a step-by-step guide to turning your own ideas and experiences into a play.

We hope these books will inspire you to study more about the craft of playwriting and to write your own play. We plan to publish a book of plays written by our readers. Please send us your play to consider for this future book. You may send it to the editors at our address, which is in the front of the book.

SELECTED FROM
DEATH OF A SALESMAN
by Arthur Miller

EDITORS' INTRODUCTION

Death of a Salesman is a drama written by Arthur Miller. It was first performed in 1949 and has been performed thousands of times since. It is considered one of the great American plays.

Death of a Salesman is about the Loman family. Most of the play takes place in their house in Brooklyn, New York. The play has scenes in both the past and present.

Willy Loman is a traveling salesman who is now 63 years old. He has worked for the same company for almost 36 years. But times have changed. The men Willy used to do business with are all gone and the new buyers don't show him any respect. Willy's company has taken away his salary and he only gets a commission when he makes a sale. He borrows money from his neighbor Charley thinking his wife, Linda, won't know he isn't getting a salary.

All his life, Willy had big dreams for himself and for his two sons, Biff and Happy. But his dreams were not based on reality and have come to nothing. Willy never made it big and now his work is disappearing. Biff and Happy are both in their thirties but neither has been successful. They are now living with Willy and Linda.

As children, Biff and Happy looked up to Willy. But something happened, long ago, to make Biff lose his respect for his father.

Willy is very depressed by what has happened in his life and has begun to act strangely. Biff thinks that this would never happen to someone like their successful neighbor Charley.

In the selection, Linda tries to get Biff and Happy to understand what is happening to their father.

DEATH OF A SALESMAN

BIFF: People are worse off than Willy Loman. Believe me, I've seen them!

LINDA: Then make Charley your father, Biff. You can't do that, can you? I don't

14

say he's a great man. Willy Loman never made a lot of money. His name was never in the paper. He's not the finest character that ever lived. But he's a human being, and a terrible thing is happening to him. So attention must be paid. He's not to be allowed to fall into his grave like an old dog. Attention, attention must be finally paid to such a person. You called him crazy—

BIFF: I didn't mean—

LINDA: No, a lot of people think he's lost his—balance. But you don't have to be very smart to know what his trouble is. The man is exhausted.

HAPPY: Sure!

LINDA: A small man can be just as exhausted as a great man. He works for a company thirty-six years this March, opens up unheard-of territories to their trademark, and now in his old age they take his salary away.

HAPPY: [Indignantly] I didn't know that, Mom.

LINDA: You never asked, my dear! Now

that you get your spending money some-
place else you don't trouble your mind
with him.

HAPPY: But I gave you money last—

LINDA: Christmas time, fifty dollars! To fix
the hot water it cost ninety-seven fifty! For
five weeks he's been on straight commission, like a beginner, an unknown!

BIFF: Those ungrateful bastards!

LINDA: Are they any worse than his sons?
When he brought them business, when he
was young, they were glad to see him. But
now his old friends, the old buyers that
loved him so and always found some order to hand him in a pinch—they're all
dead, retired. He used to be able to make
six, seven calls a day in Boston. Now he
takes his valises out of the car and puts
them back and takes them out again and
he's exhausted. Instead of walking he
talks now. He drives seven hundred miles,
and when he gets there no one knows him
any more, no one welcomes him. And
what goes through a man's mind, driving
seven hundred miles home without hav-

ing earned a cent? Why shouldn't he talk to himself? Why? When he has to go to Charley and borrow fifty dollars a week and pretend to me that it's his pay? How long can that go on? How long? You see what I'm sitting here and waiting for? And you tell me he has no character? The man who never worked a day but for your benefit? When does he get the medal for that? Is this his reward—to turn around at the age of sixty-three and find his sons, who he loved better than his life, one a philandering bum—

HAPPY: Mom!

LINDA: That's all you are, my baby! [To BIFF] And you! What happened to the love you had for him? You were such pals! How you used to talk to him on the phone every night! How lonely he was till he could come home to you!

BIFF: All right, Mom. I'll live here in my room, and I'll get a job. I'll keep away from him, that's all.

LINDA: No, Biff. You can't stay here and fight all the time.

17

BIFF: He threw me out of this house, remember that.

LINDA: Why did he do that? I never knew why.

BIFF: Because I know he's a fake and he doesn't like anybody around who knows!

LINDA: Why a fake? In what way? What do you mean?

BIFF: Just don't lay it all at my feet. It's between me and him—that's all I have to say. I'll chip in from now on. He'll settle for half my pay check. He'll be all right. I'm going to bed. [*He starts for the stairs.*]

LINDA: He won't be all right.

BIFF: [*Turning on the stairs, furiously*] I hate this city and I'll stay here. Now what do you want?

LINDA: He's dying, Biff.

SELECTED FROM
CEREMONIES IN DARK
OLD MEN
by Lonne Elder III

EDITORS' INTRODUCTION

Ceremonies in Dark Old Men *was written by
Lonne Elder III. It is set in a barbershop in
Harlem, a black neighborhood in New York
City. The time is the present.*

*Mr. Russell B. Parker runs the barbershop
but he has few customers. He spends most of
his time playing checkers. When he was
younger, Mr. Parker was a dancer in vaude-
ville shows. But his legs gave out and he had
to retire.*

*Mr. Parker has three grown children, Theo,
Bobby and Adele. They live in an apartment
over the barbershop.*

*Adele works to support her father and two
brothers. She has recently threatened that,
unless they find real jobs, she will lock all
three of them out of the building. Adele says
she doesn't want to end up like her mother,*

Doris, who worked herself to death supporting the family.

This threat angers Mr. Parker and his sons. Theo mixes up a batch of corn whiskey and the three men talk about what to do. During this discussion, Mr. Parker reminisces about his dead wife.

CEREMONIES IN DARK OLD MEN

MR. PARKER: [Pause] You know something? That woman was the first woman I ever got close to—your mama...

BOBBY: *How old were you?*

MR. PARKER: Twenty.

BOBBY: Aw, come on, Pop!

MR. PARKER: May God wipe me away from this earth...

THEO: Twenty years old and you had never touched a woman? You must've been in bad shape.

MR. PARKER: I'll tell you about it.

THEO: Here he goes with another one of his famous stories!

MR. PARKER: I can always go on upstairs, you know.

THEO: No, Pop, we want to hear it.

MR. PARKER: Well, I was working in this circus in Tampa, Florida—your mother's hometown. You remember Bob Shepard—well, we had this little dance routine of ours we used to do a sample of outside the tent. One day we was out there doing one of our numbers, when right in the middle of the number I spied this fine, foxy-looking thing, blinking her eyes at me. 'Course ol' Bob kept saying it was him she was looking at, but I knew it was *me*—'cause if there was one thing that was my specialty, it was a fine-looking woman.

THEO: You live twenty years of you life not getting anywhere near a woman, and all of a sudden they become *your* *specialty*?

MR. PARKER: Yeah, being that—

THEO: Being that you had never had a woman for all them terrible years, naturally it was on your mind all the time.

MR. PARKER: That's right.

THEO: And it being on your mind so much, you sorta became a specialist on women?

MR. PARKER: Right again.

THEO: [*Laughs*] I don't know. But I guess you got a point there!

MR. PARKER: You want to hear this or not!?

BOBBY: Yeah, go on, Pop. *I'm* listening.

MR. PARKER: Well, while I was standing on the back of the platform, I motions to her with my hand to kinda move around to the side of the stand, so I could talk to 'er. She strolled 'round to the side, stood there for a while, and you know what? Ol' Bob wouldn't let me get a word in edgewise. But you know what she told him; she said Mister, you talk like a fool! [*All laugh*]

BOBBY: That was Mama, all right.

MR. PARKER: So I asked her if she would like to meet me after the circus closed down. When I got off that night, sure enough, she was waiting for me. We walked up to the main section of town, off to the side of the road, 'cause we had a hard rain that day and the road was full of muddy little ponds. I got to talking to her and telling her funny stories and she would laugh—boy, I'm telling you that woman could laugh!

THEO: That was your technique, huh? Keep 'em laughing!

MR. PARKER: Believe it or not, it worked— 'cause she let me kiss her. I kissed her under this big ol' pecan tree. She could kiss too. When that woman kissed me, somethin' grabbed me so hard and shook me so, I fell flat on my back into a big puddle of water! *And that woman killed herself laughing!*

[Pause]

I married her two weeks later.

THEO: And then you started making up for lost time. I'm glad you did, Pop—'cause if you hadn't, I wouldn't be here today.

MR. PARKER: If I know you, you'd have made some kind of arrangement.

BOBBY: What happened after that?

MR. PARKER: We just lived and had fun—and children too, that part you know about. We lived bad and we lived good—and then my legs got wobbly, and my feet got heavy, I lost my feeling, and everything just stayed as it was.

[*Pause*]

I only wish I had been as good a haircutter as I was a dancer. Maybe she wouldn't have had to work so hard. She might be living today.

THEO: Forget it, Pop—it's all in the gone by. Come on, you need another drink. [*Pouring*]

SELECTED FROM
TORCH SONG TRILOGY
by Harvey Fierstein

EDITORS' INTRODUCTION

Torch Song Trilogy *is a comedy written by Harvey Fierstein. It takes place in New York City in the present.*

The play deals with the realities of being gay and finding love, friends and family. By presenting painful situations in a humorous light, Fierstein makes us identify and sympathize with his characters.

Arnold Beckoff is in his thirties. He and his companion, Alan, had planned to adopt a child. But soon after their decision, Alan was beaten to death by a gang of teenagers. When the agency told Arnold that a teenage boy was available for adoption, Arnold decided to try to raise the boy, David, himself.

After a trial period, Arnold is ready to proceed with the adoption. When his mother comes for a visit, Arnold realizes he must tell her the truth about his new family. Mrs. Beckoff, who is not happy with Arnold's lifestyle in general, finds the situation difficult to understand. In the selection, Arnold tries to explain his feelings to her.

The play, Torch Song Trilogy, has also been made into a movie.

TORCH SONG TRILOGY

ARNOLD: [Sits next to her, pause] Is this it? We gonna sit and stare into space?

MA: You want I should do a Bubble Dance?

ARNOLD: I need a cigarette. [He gets one.]

MA: Frankly, Arnold, you've done a lot of crazy things, but this...?

ARNOLD: Adopting David is not a crazy thing. It's a wonderful thing that I'm very proud of.

MA: If you're so proud how come you were too ashamed to tell your mother? Everything else you tell me. You shove your sex-life down my throat like aspirin; every hour on the hour. But six months he's been here and not a word. Why?

ARNOLD: I don't know.

MA: So what's new?

ARNOLD: Ma...Y'know, you're not the easiest person in the world to talk to.

MA: What did I say? Do I tell you how to run your life? Let me tell you something, my son: I learned long ago that no matter what I said or how I felt you and your brother were going to do just as you pleased anyway. So, I wouldn't say a word. On purpose! You want to know why you didn't tell me about this? I'll tell you why: Because you knew it was wrong.

ARNOLD: That's not true.

MA: No?

ARNOLD: No!

MA: Why then?

ARNOLD: ...I don't know.

MA: You would if you'd listen.

ARNOLD: This isn't something I decided to do overnight. We put in our application more than two years ago.

MA: Who "we"?

ARNOLD: Alan and I.

MA: The two of you were going to do this together?

ARNOLD: That was the idea.

MA: Now I've heard everything.

ARNOLD: That's what I love about you; you're so open minded.

MA: All right. So, Alan's not here. Why's the kid?

ARNOLD: Because with everything else I forgot about the application. Then, one day, the phone rang. It was the foster parent program and they had David for us. I told them what happened to Alan and they said I could probably take David anyway.

MA: And you said, "send him on over."

ARNOLD: Not at first. But then I thought it all through, called them back and said yes. . . . On a trial basis.

MA: I'm glad you got a money-back guarantee, but you still haven't told me why you wanted him.

ARNOLD: Because I was tired of widowing.

MA: Wida-whating?

ARNOLD: Widowing. Widow-ing. It's a word of Murray's.

MA: And a nice one at that. What does it mean?

ARNOLD: You know.

MA: No, I don't know.

ARNOLD: Widowing...feeling sorry for myself, cursing every time I passed a couple walking hand in hand, watching Tear Jerkers on TV knowing they could only cheer me up. Christ, of all the things going down here, I was sure that was the one thing I wouldn't have to explain.

MA: How should I know about Whatchamacallit? Did you ever say a word to me?

ARNOLD: I didn't think I had to. Christ, it's only been three years since daddy died.

MA: Wait, wait, wait, wait, wait. Are you trying to compare my marriage with you and Alan? [*Haughty and incensed*] Your father and I were married for thirty-five years, had two children and a wonderful life together. You have the nerve to compare yourself to that?

ARNOLD: [*Scared*] That's not what I mean, I'm talking about the loss.

MA: What loss did you have? You fooled around with some boy . . . ? Where do you come to compare that to a marriage of thirty-five years?

ARNOLD: You think it doesn't?

MA: Come on, Arnold. You think you're talking to one of your pals?

ARNOLD: Ma, I lost someone that I loved very much . . .

MA: So you felt bad. Maybe you cried a little. But what would you know about what I went through? Thirty-five years I lived with that man. He got sick, I brought him to the hospital and you know what they gave me back? I gave them a man . . . they gave me a paper bag with his watch, wallet and wedding ring. How could you possibly know what that felt like. It took me two months until I could sleep in our bed alone, a year to learn to say "I" instead of "we." And you're going to tell me you were "widowing." How dare you!

ARNOLD: You're right, Ma. How dare I. I couldn't possibly know how it feels to pack someone's clothes in plastic bags and watch the garbage pickers carry them away. Or what it feels like to forget and set his place at the table. How about the food that rots in the refrigerator because you forgot how to shop for one? How dare I? Right, Ma? How dare I?

MA: [Starting over his speech and continuing until her exit] May God strike me dead! Whatever I did to my mother to deserve a child speaking to me this way. The disrespect! I only pray that one day you have a son and that he'll talk to you like this. The way you talk to me.

ARNOLD: [Over her speech] Listen, Ma, you had it easy. You have thirty-five years to remember, I have five. You had your children and friends to comfort you, I had me! My friends didn't want to hear about it. They said, "What're you gripin' about? At least you had a lover." 'Cause everybody knows that queers don't love. How dare I? You had it easy, Ma. You lost your husband in a nice clean hospital, I lost mine out there. They killed him there on the street. Twenty-three years old laying dead on the street. Killed by a bunch of kids with baseball bats. [MA *has fled the room.* ARNOLD *continues to rant.*] Children. Children taught by people like you. 'Cause everybody knows that queers don't matter! Queers don't love! And those that do deserve what they get! [*He stops, catches his breath, sits down.*] Whatever happened to good ole' American Momism and apple pie?

SELECTED FROM
CRIMES OF THE HEART
by Beth Henley

EDITORS' INTRODUCTION

Crimes of the Heart is a comedy written by Beth Henley. It takes place in the kitchen of the Magrath sisters' home in Hazlehurst, Mississippi, a small southern town. The time is autumn in the recent past. Henley takes complicated family situations and makes them funny through her characters' words.

The Magrath sisters are Lenny, 30 years old, Meg, 27, and Babe, 24. They are together again for the first time in five years. The sisters were brought up by their grandparents.

Lenny lives in the family home where she has spent many years caring for their grandfather. He is now ill and in the hospital.

Babe is staying with Lenny. She is out on bail because she shot and nearly killed her husband, Zackery. They had an unhappy marriage and Zackery discovered Babe was having an affair with a 15-year-old black boy.

Meg has come home to help Babe. She had

gone to Hollywood many years earlier hoping to become a famous singer and actress.

Lenny and Meg have just been to visit their grandfather. It is Lenny's birthday.

The play, Crimes of the Heart, has also been made into a movie.

CRIMES OF THE HEART

LENNY enters. She is fuming. BABE is rolling her hair throughout most of the following scene.

BABE: Lenny, hi!

LENNY: Hi.

BABE: Where's Meg?

LENNY: Oh, she had to go by the store and pick some things up. I don't know what.

BABE: Well, how's Old Granddaddy?

LENNY: [As she picks up BABE's bowl of oatmeal] He's fine. Wonderful! Never been better!

BABE: Lenny, what's wrong? What's the matter?

LENNY: It's Meg! I could just wring her neck! I could just wring it!

BABE: Why? Wha'd she do?

LENNY: She lied! She sat in that hospital room and shamelessly lied to Old Granddaddy. She went on and on telling such untrue stories and lies.

BABE: Well, what? What did she say?

LENNY: Well, for one thing, she said she was gonna have an RCA record coming out with her picture on the cover, eating pineapples under a palm tree.

BABE: Well, gosh, Lenny, maybe she is! Don't you think she really is?

LENNY: Babe, she sat here this very afternoon and told me how all that she's done this whole year is work as a clerk for a dog-food company.

BABE: Oh, shoot. I'm disappointed.

LENNY: And then she goes on to say that she'll be appearing on the Johnny Carson show in two weeks' time. Two weeks' time! Why, Old Granddaddy's got a TV set right in his room. Imagine what a letdown it's gonna be.

BABE: Why, mercy me.

LENNY: [Slamming the coffeepot on] Oh, and she told him the reason she didn't use the money he sent her to come home Christmas was that she was right in the middle of making a huge multimillion-dollar motion picture and was just under too much pressure.

BABE: My word!

LENNY: The movie's coming out this spring. It's called, *Singing in a Shoe Factory*. But she only has a small leading role—not a large leading role.

BABE: [Laughing] For heaven's sake—

LENNY: I'm sizzling. Oh, I just can't help it! I'm sizzling!

BABE: Sometimes Meg does such strange things.

LENNY: [Slowly, as she picks up the opened box of birthday candy] Who ate this candy?

BABE: [Hesitantly] Meg.

LENNY: My one birthday present, and look what she does! Why, she's taken one little bite out of each piece and then just put it back in! Ooh! That's just like her! That is just like her!

BABE: Lenny, please—

LENNY: I can't help it! It gets me mad! It gets me upset! Why, Meg's always run wild—she started smoking and drinking when she was fourteen years old; she never made good grades—never made her own bed! But somehow she always seemed to get what she wanted. She's the one who got singing and dancing lessons, and a store-bought dress to wear to her senior prom. Why, do you remember how Meg always got to wear twelve jingle bells on her petticoats, while we were only allowed to wear three apiece? Why?! Why should Old Grandmama let her sew twelve golden jingle bells on her petticoats and us only three!

BABE: [*Who has heard all this before*] I don't know! Maybe she didn't jingle them as much!

LENNY: I can't help it! It gets me mad! I resent it. I do.

SELECTED FROM
THE GUITARRÓN
by Lynne Alvarez

EDITORS' INTRODUCTION

The Guitarrón is a drama written by Lynne Alvarez. It takes place along the beach in Veracruz, Mexico, in the present time.

Guitarrón is Spanish for the musical instrument, the cello. In the play, the cello is played by an old man known only as the Maestro. Maestro is a term of respect for a master musician. The Maestro is a larger-than-life character. He seems to have great knowledge and understanding. His music seems to give him powers over people and events.

The Maestro plays his cello, day and night, on the beach. This particular beach belongs to the federal government, so the local police do not patrol it. At night, it is a dangerous place, full of criminals and drug dealers.

Guicho is a 17-year-old boy. He both admires and fears the Maestro. Yet Guicho has told him the name of the young woman he loves, Micaela.

In the selection, Guicho seeks out the Maestro at night on the beach to talk about his love.

THE GUITARRÓN

GUICHO *is sprinting along the beach after seeing* MICAELA. *He can hardly contain his excitement.*

The MAESTRO *is playing on top of a dune. It is midnight.*

We can't hear the MAESTRO *at first, but as* GUICHO *approaches him the sound increases in volume. When* GUICHO *addresses him, the* MAESTRO *stops.*

GUICHO: Maestro.

MAESTRO: Oh it's you.

GUICHO: An old man like you shouldn't be out here on the beach alone.

MAESTRO: And a young man like you?

GUICHO: This ain't a tourist beach. You could get yourself into trouble.

MAESTRO: Oh there's always the police, don't you think? I imagine a scream or two would bring them running.

GUICHO: The police won't come here. It's a federal zone. Only the army can come and they don't bother with us...unless they want dope. What you doing out here anyways? It's dangerous.

MAESTRO: I agree. But it wouldn't be quite so beautiful without danger, don't you think? Soft waves, a sea breeze, salt in the air...utterly forgettable without that sharp edge of malice. Brings me alive, reminds me one never knows what will happen next! Delightful.

GUICHO: I'll walk you to the street if you like. I ain't tired at all.

MAESTRO: And I'm not tired either. We're in the same mood, no doubt. In love.

GUICHO: You got a girlfriend?

MAESTRO: Don't be so incredulous, young man. [*Holds out the cello*] Isn't this shaped like a woman? And I make her tremble when I touch her so. [*He passes the bow over the strings.*]

GUICHO: I thought you were talking about a girl...a woman.

MAESTRO: There are loves beyond women.

GUICHO: Not for me, señor. And it's more than love. It's passion!

MAESTRO: Passion. Of course, she's beautiful, wonderful, a cornucopia of delights!

GUICHO: She can kill me with a look!

MAESTRO: Well, well, well, we have a common language. Passion is my daily bread.

GUICHO: An old man like you.

MAESTRO: I measure passion by foolhardiness, young man. And what could be more foolhardy than a rich old man sneaking out to play alone at midnight on a beach infested with...criminals! You may feel you're risking your heart for a mere glance from this girl, but I am risking my life for one moment of beautiful music on a beach at midnight! That's passion.

[GUICHO *laughs and sits down at the* MAESTRO's *feet.*]

GUICHO: You can keep playing if you like. It's nice out.

MAESTRO: You'll stand guard, eh?

GUICHO: Sure.

MAESTRO: Thank you. But you had bette
leave.

GUICHO: I like it here.

MAESTRO: It's dangerous. [GUICHO *laughs.*
I'm dangerous.

GUICHO: Are you kidding? I could snap
you in two like a twig, old man . . .

MAESTRO: Of course, you see danger a
clubbing someone on the head, don't you
Go away and be happy with your young
woman!

GUICHO: There's no way you could be
dangerous to me. No way!

MAESTRO: Then why are you up in arms
your back bristling, your heart pumping
fire? [*He laughs.*] When I say something
you don't understand, you feel threat
ened, look at you.

GUICHO: I was just wondering.

MAESTRO: You'll do more than wonder
You'll remember.

SELECTED FROM
A WASTED WEEKEND
(an episode of *Hill Street Blues*)
by David Mamet

EDITORS' INTRODUCTION

A Wasted Weekend *was written by David Mamet as an episode for the popular television series,* Hill Street Blues. *The action in the script takes place inside and outside the police station featured in the show.*

A script written for television or the movies is different from one for the stage. Because the action is seen through the "eyes" of the cameras, the writer can let us see as much or as little of what is happening as he wants. Because many pieces of film are edited together to make the final show, he can cut quickly from the point of view of one camera to that of another. In a screenplay, the writer tells us more than where the scene takes place (using words such as "Interior" or "Exterior") and what the actors are to do. He also tells us what the cameras will film for the audience to see by describing the "angle" of the shots.

When the writer doesn't want a quick cut, he may tell the camera to "hold" on a shot.

Mamet sometimes tells the actors to wait a "beat" before they react or speak, to emphasize the humor in a situation.

The selection takes place inside one hunting cabin and outside another cabin. Police officers Jablonski, Hill and Renko are on a hunting trip. John Swoboda, a friend of Jablonski, has lent them his cabin for the weekend. When they arrive, they can't find the keys to the cabin so they break in and make themselves at home.

A WASTED WEEKEND
[an episode of *Hill Street Blues*]

Interior: Sumptuous hunting cabin. Evening.

Classical soft music on the stereo. A fire in the huge fieldstone fireplace. JABLONSKI, HILL *and* RENKO *playing poker at a huge, oak-slab table.*

JABLONSKI: Two cards.

HILL: [Dealing] Two cards ...

RENKO: Similarly ...

HILL: Two cards for the man, and the dealer takes one ...

RENKO: ... frontin' off as usual.

HILL: And time will tell. And, Stan, I believe that it is your bet.

[Sound of a key in the lock. All heads turn.]

ANGLE POINT OF VIEW: The front door of the cabin opening. A man and a woman come in, necking furiously. Hold on the necking.

ANGLE: The men at the poker table, looking on.

ANGLE: The necking couple maneuvering themselves, entwined, toward the couch and the men at the table looking on for a long time. Finally RENKO clears his throat. He clears his throat again.

RENKO: [To JABLONSKI] Is that your guy??? [JABLONSKI shakes his head.]

JABLONSKI: Sir ... ?

[*The necking man looks up. Beat. He jumps back away from the disheveled, half-clothed woman. He starts dressing himself.*]

GUY: What are, you, who are, what you doing here . . . ?

[*The* GUY *starts trying to get a hunting rifle off of its moorings on the wall. The cops stand.*]

HILL: It's, it's, hold on, we're police officers . . . !!! HOLD IT!!! HOLD IT!!!

[JABLONSKI *and* HILL *are fumbling out their badges. The* GUY *continues to try to get the rifle off the wall.* RENKO *takes out his revolver and holds it up.*]

RENKO: I said hold it, for God's sake:

[*Beat. The* GUY *puts down the rifle.*]

Now, who are you?

GUY: Who are you?

JABLONSKI: We're friends of John Swoboda.

[*Beat*]

GUY: And who is John Swoboda?

[*Beat*]

HILL: Uh, is this John Swoboda's cabin?

GUY: No, it is not. It's *my* cabin.

HILL: And you are . . . ?

GUY: Who *I* am, it's none of your *business* who I am. You're in my home . . . what did, you're *police* officers . . . ???

RENKO: Yessir.

GUY: Well, then I think that you'd better give me your names and badge numbers.

JABLONSKI: Um, um, sir, could I *talk* to you a moment . . . could I talk *with* you a moment, please?

[JABLONSKI *goes off to the corner, leaving* RENKO, HILL *and the disheveled young woman. Beat*]

RENKO: We are *awful* sorry to have, as it seems we have, broken into . . .

HILL: None of us have *been* here before, and we'll certainly . . .

RENKO: Any *damages* that . . .

JABLONSKI: Pack it up, lads, and let's move on. We want the next cabin down.

[HILL *and* RENKO *hurriedly assemble*

their belongings and apologize themselves out of the door.]

HILL: We're incredibly sorry.

RENKO: An honest misunderstanding, any damages, we'll certainly . . .

CAMERA follows the three men out of the door, foodstuffs, rifles, hunting gear in their arms. They go over to the station wagon and they put their stuff in the station wagon. They start to drive down the dirt road.

HILL: How did you talk us out of that . . . ?

JABLONSKI: Guy had a wedding ring on, the woman did not. [*Beat*]

RENKO: I thought he didn't kiss her like the two of them were married.

JABLONSKI: So it seems we're *all* of us going to forgive and forget.

HILL: So if we got the wrong place, then how is Henry going to find us?

RENKO: And where is our hunting lodge . . . ?

[*The car pulls up outside a hovel.*]

Angle Exterior: The hovel.

Dark against the night sky. It is a falling down shack. The men get out.

JABLONSKI: Does anybody want to chop some wood . . . ?

SELECTED FROM
FRANKIE AND JOHNNY
IN THE CLAIR DE LUNE
by Terrence McNally

EDITORS' INTRODUCTION

Frankie and Johnny in the Clair de Lune is a dramatic comedy written by Terrence McNally. The play has only two characters—Frankie and Johnny. It takes place in Frankie's one-room New York City apartment in the present time.

Frankie is a waitress at a nearby diner where Johnny is a cook. They are both middle-aged.

Although they have known one another for a while, they have just gone on their first date. Now, they are in Frankie's apartment. They have just made love while the radio played beautiful piano music.

Johnny tells Frankie he loves her. Frankie thinks Johnny is moving too fast for her and asks him to leave. When he refuses, she says she is going out and he had better be gone

when she gets back. She is just about to leave
as the selection begins.

Johnny is on the telephone. To keep Fran-
kie from leaving, Johnny calls the radio sta-
tion to stall for time and to find out the name
of the beautiful music that was playing. He
then asks the disc jockey to play the most
beautiful music ever written, just for them.
The piece the disc jockey chooses is called
"Clair de Lune" by Debussy. Clair de lune
means moonlight in French.

Music is very important to this play. Even
the characters' names refer to music—"Fran-
kie and Johnny" is the title of an old popular
song with the first line: "Frankie and Johnny
were lovers."

The play, Frankie and Johnny in the Clair
de Lune, has been made into the movie, Fran-
kie and Johnny.

FRANKIE AND JOHNNY IN THE CLAIR DE LUNE

JOHNNY: [*Into phone*] May I speak to your
disc jockey? . . . Well excuse me! [*He cov-*
ers phone, to FRANKIE] They don't have a

disc jockey. They have someone called Midnight With Marlon. [*Into phone*] Hello, Marlon? My name is Johnny. My friend and I were making love and in the afterglow, which I sometimes think is the most beautiful part of making love, she noticed that you were playing some really beautiful music, piano. She was right. I don't know much about quality music, which I could gather that was, so I would like to know the name of that particular piece and the artist performing it so I can buy the record and present it to my lady love, whose name is Frankie and is that a beautiful coincidence or is it not? [*Short pause*] Bach. Johann Sebastian, right? I heard of him. The Goldberg Variations. Glenn Gould. Columbia Records. [*To* FRANKIE] You gonna remember this? [FRANKIE *smacks him hard across the cheek.* JOHNNY *takes the phone from his ear and holds it against his chest. He just looks at her. She smacks him again. This time he catches her hand while it is still against his cheek, holds it a beat, then brings it to his lips and kisses it. Then, into phone, he continues but what he says is really for* FRANKIE, *his eyes never leaving her.*] Do you take requests, Marlon? Then make an exception! There's a man and a woman. Not young, not old. No great beauties, either one. They meet where they work: a restaurant and it's not the Ritz. She's a waitress. He's a cook. They meet but they don't connect. "I got two medium burgers working" and "Pick up, side of fries" is pretty much the extent of it. But she's noticed him, he can feel it. And he's noticed her. Right off. They both knew tonight was going to happen. So why did it take him six weeks for him to ask her if she wanted to see a movie that neither one of them could tell you the name of right now? Why did they eat ice cream sundaes before she asked him if he wanted to come up since they were in the neighborhood? And then they were making love and for maybe an hour they forgot the ten million things that made them think "I don't love this person. I don't even like them" and instead all they knew was that they were together and it was perfect and they were perfect and that's all there was to know about it and as they lay there, they both began the million reasons not to love one another like a familiar rosary. Only this time he stopped himself. Maybe it was the music you were playing. They both heard it. Only now they're both beginning to forget they did. So would you play something for Frankie and Johnny on the eve of something that ought to last, not self-destruct. I guess I want you to play the most beautiful music ever written and dedicate it to us. [*He hangs up.*] Don't go.

FRANKIE: Why are you doing this?

JOHNNY: I'm tired of looking. Everything I want is in this room.

SELECTED FROM
DO THE RIGHT THING
by Spike Lee

EDITORS' INTRODUCTION

Do the Right Thing *is Spike Lee's screenplay for his successful movie. He not only wrote the screenplay but produced, directed and starred in the movie. Spike Lee got the idea for this movie from a racial incident that happened in New York City.*

Screenplays have different directions than plays written for the stage. You can learn about some of these differences in the Editors' Introduction to "Selected from A Wasted Weekend." *The screenplay of* Do the Right Thing *also directs the cameraman to film "close-ups." In a close-up shot, the expressions on the actors' faces as well as what they say help us understand their thoughts and feelings.*

Do the Right Thing *takes place in a mostly black neighborhood in Brooklyn, New York. There has been a heat wave and all the action* takes place on the hottest day of the year. Tempers are short and people are angry.

The movie's central character is Mookie, a young black man who works in Sal's Famous Pizzeria. Sal, an Italian-American, has been in business in the neighborhood for many years. His two sons, Pino and Vito, work with Sal but they think he should move the business to their own white neighborhood. Tensions are spreading in this neighborhood between blacks, whites, asians, west indians and hispanics and between the police and the people.

In the selection, Mookie's friend Buggin' Out comes into Sal's for a slice of pizza. He focuses on the main decoration in the pizzeria, Sal's Wall of Fame, a wall decorated with photographs of famous Italian-Americans.

DO THE RIGHT THING

Interior: Sal's Famous Pizzeria. Day.

Customers are in Sal's; it's lunch time and it's fairly busy. SAL puts a hot slice

down on the counter in front of BUGGIN'
OUT, a b-boy.

SAL: You paying now or on layaway?
[BUGGIN' OUT looks at the slice.]

BUGGIN' OUT: How much?

SAL: You come in here at least three times
a day. You a retard? A buck fifty.

BUGGIN' OUT: Damn, Sal, put some more
cheese on that motherfucker.

SAL: Extra cheese is two dollars. Y'know
dat.

BUGGIN' OUT: Two dollars! Forget it.
[BUGGIN' OUT slams his money down on
the counter, takes his slice and sits
down.]

ANGLE: Table

[All around BUGGIN' OUT, peering down
from the Wall of Fame, are signed,
framed, eight by ten glossies of famous
Italian-Americans. WE SEE Joe Di-
Maggio, Rocky Marciano, Perry Como,
Frank Sinatra, Luciano Pavarotti, Liza
Minnelli, Governor Mario Cuomo, Al

Pacino and, of course, how can we for-get Sylvester Stallone as Rocky Balboa: The Italian Stallion, also Rambo.]

CLOSE-UP: BUGGIN' OUT

[*He looks at the pictures hovering above him.*]

BUGGIN' OUT: Mookie.

CLOSE-UP: MOOKIE

MOOKIE: What?

CLOSE-UP: BUGGIN' OUT

BUGGIN' OUT: How come you ain't got no brothers up?

CLOSE-UP: MOOKIE

MOOKIE: Ask Sal.

ANGLE: Pizzeria

BUGGIN' OUT: Sal, how come you ain't got no brothers up on the wall here?

SAL: You want brothers up on the Wall of Fame, you open up your own business, then you can do what you wanna do. My pizzeria, Italian-Americans up on the wall.

VITO: Take it easy, Pop.

SAL: Don't start on me today.

BUGGIN' OUT: Sal, that might be fine, you own this, but rarely do I see any *Italian-Americans* eating in here. All I've ever seen is Black folks. So since we spend much money here, we do have some say.

SAL: You a troublemaker?

[PINO walks over to BUGGIN' OUT.]

PINO: You making trouble.

BUGGIN' OUT: Put some brothers up on this Wall of Fame. We want Malcolm X, Angela Davis, Michael Jordan tomorrow.

[SAL *comes from behind the counter with his Louisville Slugger Mickey Mantle model baseball bat.* VITO *is by his side, but* MOOKIE *intercepts them, and takes* BUGGIN' OUT *outside.*]

SAL: Don't come back, either.

BUGGIN' OUT: Boycott Sal's. Boycott Sal's.

AN INTERVIEW WITH ARTHUR MILLER, PLAYWRIGHT

*On March 5, 1991, Arthur Miller talked
with the learners, volunteers and staff of
Literacy Volunteers of New York City. He
answered questions about himself and his
writing.*

QUESTION: Why did you become a writer?

MR. MILLER: One reason is that my mother
loved books. There were a lot of books
around the house. I got the idea from her
that being a writer was praiseworthy and
a very good thing to be. That was the beginning.

But, like a lot of kids, I was always telling stories. And I was always inventing
things that were better than the truth.
There's an impulse, in some people, to
create a world that doesn't exist. And to
live in one's imagination. Literature al-
lows a writer to do that.

QUESTION: How did you get interested in writing plays?

MR. MILLER: My father was almost illiterate. He could just barely read a newspaper. But he had a big business and he was very good at faking it. He loved the theater—he loved to hear language since he couldn't read it.

QUESTION: How do you invent a character like Willy Loman?

MR. MILLER: A play comes from many different sources. I never knew anyone exactly like Willy Loman but I knew a lot of salesmen. They all fed into the character. I put together impressions and ideas I had about people.

QUESTION: Do you like your characters?

MR. MILLER: You can't create a character that is believable if you don't feel very close and sympathetic with him. You might not like the character but you have to share his or her emotions.

QUESTION: How do you make a character talk like a real person?

61

MR. MILLER: The character's feelings have to come through his words so you can begin to believe them, to see the truth about the person. To arrive at that, you have to start with the language.

I always listened to the way people spoke. It's good exercise, really listening to what people are saying. You can tell a lot about them. I think I got some of this listening ability from my father. Because he couldn't read, he listened very carefully.

Being a writer, you have to be open to everything coming at you, wherever it's coming from, whatever kind of person is talking. We hear something and want to re-create it but with a different background. A writer re-creates the language to provide insight into a character and his story.

QUESTION: How long does it take you to write a play?

MR. MILLER: It usually takes me six months to two years to write a play. But recently I finished a play that I started eight years ago. I tried to finish it four times. I think I must have written about 2,000 pages to get the 120 pages that are the finished play. It took time.

QUESTION: Do you find it hard to edit your writing?

MR. MILLER: Yes, because you fall in love with some of your writing just because you wrote it. But you know it should be taken out, even if it's hard to do. I throw away more than I keep.

QUESTION: Do you have any advice for new writers?

MR. MILLER: There are no short cuts that I know of. Some people can write with great ease and they are blessed. I can't do that. The only advice I can give to writers is to tell the truth as you know it. And that often takes a lot of work.

Three series of good books for all readers:

Writers' Voices—A multicultural, whole-language series books offering selections from some of America's finest write along with background information, maps, glossaries, questic and activities and many more supplementary materials for reade Our list of authors includes: Amy Tan • Alex Haley • Al Walker • Rudolfo Anaya • Louise Erdrich • Oscar Hijuelo Maxine Hong Kingston • Gloria Naylor • Anne Tyler • T Wolfe • Mario Puzo • Avery Corman • Judith Krantz • La McMurtry • Mary Higgins Clark • Stephen King • Peter Be chley • Ray Bradbury • Sidney Sheldon • Maya Angelo Jane Goodall • Mark Mathabane • Loretta Lynn • Kather Jackson • Carol Burnett • Kareem Abdul-Jabbar • Ted W liams • Ahmad Rashad • Abigail Van Buren • Priscilla Pr ley • Paul Monette • Robert Fulghum • Bill Cosby • Luci Clifton • Robert Bly • Robert Frost • Nikki Giovanni • Lan; ton Hughes • Joy Harjo • Edna St. Vincent Millay • Willia Carlos Williams • Terrence McNally • Jules Feiffer • Alfi Uhry • Horton Foote • Marsha Norman • Lynne Alvarez Lonne Elder III • ntozake shange • Neil Simon • August W son • Harvey Fierstein • Beth Henley • David Mamet • Arti Miller and Spike Lee.

New Writers' Voices—A series of anthologies and individ narratives by talented new writers. Stories, poems and true I experiences written by adult learners cover such topics as heal home and family, love, work, facing challenges and life in forei countries. Many *New Writers' Voices* contain photographs a illustrations.

Reference—A reference library for adult new readers and write The first two books in the series are *How to Write a Play* a *Discovering Words: The Stories Behind English*.

Write for our free complete catalog:
LVNYC Publishing Program
121 Avenue of the Americas
New York, New York 10013